PAPER CRAFTS
FOR
THANKSGIVING

Randel McGee

Enslow Elementary

an imprint of

Enslow Publishers, Inc.
40 Industrial Road
Box 398
Berkeley Heights, NJ 07922
USA

http://www.enslow.com

Dedicated to my wife, my children, and their families.
How thankful I am for them!

"Live in thanksgiving daily."(Book of Mormon | Alma 34:38)

This book meets the National Standards for Arts Education.

Enslow Elementary, an imprint of Enslow Publishers, Inc.
Enslow Elementary® is a registered trademark of Enslow Publishers, Inc.

Library of Congress Cataloging-in-Publication Data

McGee, Randel.
    Paper crafts for Thanksgiving / Randel McGee.
       p. cm. — (Paper craft fun for holidays)
    Includes bibliographical references and index.
    Summary: "Explains the significance of Thanksgiving and how to make Thanksgiving-themed crafts out of paper"—
       Provided by publisher.
    ISBN 978-0-7660-3722-9
    1. Thanksgiving decorations—Juvenile literature. 2. Paper work—Juvenile literature. I. Title.
    TT900.T5M35 2012
    745.594'1—dc22
                 2010013615

Paperback ISBN: 978-1-59845-336-2

Printed in the United States of America

052011 Lake Book Manufacturing, Inc., Melrose Park, IL

10 9 8 7 6 5 4 3 2 1

To Our Readers: We have done our best to make sure all Internet Addresses in this book were active and appropriate when we went to press. However, the author and the publisher have no control over and assume no liability for the material available on those Internet sites or on other Web sites they may link to. Any comments or suggestions can be sent by e-mail to comments@enslow.com or to the address on the back cover.

Every effort has been made to locate all copyright holders of material used in this book. If any errors or omissions have occurred, corrections will be made in future editions of this book.

♻ Enslow Publishers, Inc., is committed to printing our books on recycled paper. The paper in every book contains 10% to 30% post-consumer waste (PCW). The cover board on the outside of each book contains 100% PCW. Our goal is to do our part to help young people and the environment too!

Illustration Credits: Crafts prepared by Randel McGee; photography by Nicole diMella/Enslow Publishers, Inc., except © Randel McGee, p. 23, and Shutterstock, p. 5.

Cover Illustration: Crafts prepared by Randel McGee; photography by Nicole diMella/Enslow Publishers, Inc.

CONTENTS

AUTHOR'S NOTE: Many of the materials used in making these crafts may be found by using recycled paper products. The author uses such recycled items as cereal boxes and similar packaging for light cardboard, manila folders for card stock paper, leftover pieces of wrapping paper, and so forth. This not only reduces the cost of the projects but is also a great way to reuse and recycle paper. Be sure to ask an adult for permission before using any recycled paper products.

The projects in this book were created for this particular holiday. However, I invite readers to be imaginative and find new ways to use the ideas in this book to create different projects of their own. Please feel free to share pictures of your work with me through www.mcgeeproductions.com. Happy Crafting!

THANKSGIVING!

Thanksgiving Day in the United States is a special holiday. On the fourth Thursday of November, family, relatives, and friends gather together to feast in celebration of the things they are thankful for throughout the year. Most families have their own favorite foods on the menu, but some common Thanksgiving foods are roast turkey, cranberry sauce, sweet potatoes, and pumpkin pie. What is the story behind our Thanksgiving holiday?

The first Thanksgiving feast was celebrated in 1621 by the English settlers of Plymouth Colony in Massachusetts. The settlers were a religious group called Separatists or Pilgrims. A pilgrim is someone who travels far for religious reasons. In 1620, the Pilgrims left Europe for America to find a place to practice their religion freely. They crossed the ocean and arrived at Plymouth in a ship called the *Mayflower*.

In the fall of 1621, the Pilgrims feasted for three days with their American Indian friends. The Wampanoag (pronounced wamp-a-NO-ag) and other tribes had helped them plant crops, fish, and hunt for food.

They may have had some wild turkey to eat, but they also would have had venison (deer meat), ducks, geese, lobsters, oysters, fish, beans, carrots, squash, and corn pudding. They did not celebrate a day of Thanksgiving at the same time every year after that.

It was over two hundred years after the Pilgrims' first feast that a woman named Sarah Hale thought that there should be a national day of Thanksgiving. She wrote letters to friends and leaders around the country asking to make a national Thanksgiving holiday on the last Thursday of November. She wrote thousands of letters over seventeen years. In 1863, President Abraham Lincoln finally accepted Mrs. Hale's proposal and declared the last Thursday in November a national day of Thanksgiving. In 1941, President Franklin D. Roosevelt officially signed into law a resolution proposed by Congress that changed the date to the fourth Thursday of November.

Americans still remember the Pilgrims and American Indian friends on Thanksgiving Day, but we have added other traditions to this holiday, such as parades and sporting events. However, it is especially a time to give thanks for those people, comforts, and foods that we have that make our lives happy, safe, and healthy.

TURKEY POP-UP CARD

The turkey has become a symbol of Thanksgiving. Wild turkey may have been one of the many foods eaten during the first Thanksgiving. Roast turkey is still popular for Thanksgiving meals today. Benjamin Franklin, one of the Founding Fathers of the United States, wanted the turkey to be the national bird instead of the bald eagle. Make this turkey pop-up card to send to a friend or to use as a decoration.

WHAT YOU WILL NEED

- white card stock
- construction paper (9 x 12 inches)
- pencil
- tracing paper
- scissors
- markers or crayons
- craft foam
- white glue
- red tissue paper

WHAT TO DO

1. Fold a sheet of white card stock in half lengthwise. Fold a sheet of construction paper in half width-wise, like a book.

2. Use tracing paper to transfer the turkey patterns from page 39 to the folded card stock and cut out the patterns.

3. Take the turkey head pattern and fold back and forth on the dotted lines. Spread the turkey head pattern out flat. Gently push up on the fold lines and pinch the creases to make the beak stand out.

4. Open all the folded pattern pieces and color them as you wish.

5. On the uncolored side of each pattern piece, glue small strips of craft foam near two outside edges of the piece. Let dry.

6. Line up the crease in the tail pattern with the crease in the construction paper and glue it in place on the craft foam strip. Stack the pieces of the turkey pattern on top of each other with a drop of white glue on the craft foam strips. Let dry.

7. Glue a small piece of red tissue paper to the beak for the turkey's wattle.

8. Write a Thanksgiving greeting on the outside and inside of the card.

PILGRIM BOY AND GIRL

We often see pictures of the Pilgrims wearing black clothes and tall hats. The Pilgrims did wear black clothes for church meetings, but on most days they wore garments of light brown, red, blue, green, and even purple. Boys wore breeches (pants that came to below the knee), shirts, doublets (jacket-like vests), and hats or stocking caps. Girls wore petticoats under ankle-length skirts, blouses, aprons, and caps or bonnets.

WHAT YOU WILL NEED

- ✎ pencil
- ✎ tracing paper
- ✎ computer paper
- ✎ markers or crayons
- ✎ scissors

WHAT TO DO

1. Use the pencil and tracing paper to transfer the patterns from page 40 to the computer paper.

2. Decorate the figures as you wish.

3. Cut out the patterns.

4. Use the figures to decorate for Thanksgiving Day.

American Indian Boy and Girl

The Wampanoag people lived in the area that is now part of the states of Massachusetts and Rhode Island. The word *Wampanoag* means "people of the east." They lived in villages in small shelters called wetus. The shelters were made of poles bent and tied together and covered with large sheets of birchbark. Wampanoag children wore clothes of soft leather decorated with shells, carved bone, and beads.

What you will need

- pencil
- tracing paper
- computer paper
- markers or crayons
- scissors

WHAT TO DO

1. Use a pencil and tracing paper to transfer the patterns from page 41 to the computer paper.

2. Decorate the figures as you wish.

3. Cut out the pattern.

4. Use the figures to decorate for Thanksgiving Day.

"Happy Thanksgiving" Table Greeting

What you will need

- pencil
- tracing paper
- card stock
- markers or crayons
- scissors
- construction paper—assorted colors
- old magazines (ask permission first)
- white glue
- clear tape

In the fall of 1621, the fifty-three Pilgrims of Plymouth Colony had harvested and gathered enough food to last them well through the harsh winter. They welcomed the Wampanoag to a feast to celebrate their good fortune. Chief Massasoit and ninety members of his tribe came to join the Pilgrims. Welcome your friends and family with this colorful decoration!

WHAT TO DO

1. Use tracing paper and a pencil to transfer the two patterns from page 43 to the card stock.

2. Use markers or crayons to color in the letters.

3. Cut around the letters on the solid black lines.

4. Fold both the card stock pieces along the dotted lines to form two tents. The letters will stick up above the fold.

5. Decorate the piece with construction paper fruits and vegetables (patterns on page 43) or with food photos from old magazines or clip art programs.

6. Tape the folded card stock pieces to a construction paper base.

TURKEY STENCIL

The wild turkey is found all over North America. It is a strong flyer, but it prefers to spend its time on the ground scratching for seeds and insects. A male turkey will "show off" by fluffing up his feathers and spreading his tail to make himself look larger. A stencil is a design cut into cardboard or plastic that can be used to make copies of the design. This turkey stencil can be used to decorate all kinds of fun Thanksgiving crafts and tasty foods.

WHAT YOU WILL NEED

- pencil
- tracing paper
- light cardboard
- scissors
- markers or crayons
- watercolor paints
- paintbrush
- powdered sugar (optional)

WHAT TO DO

1. Use a pencil and tracing paper to transfer the pattern from page 38 to the light cardboard.

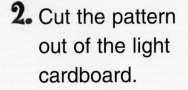

2. Cut the pattern out of the light cardboard.

3. Use markers or crayons to trace the stencil design on place mats and color in the design as you wish.

4. Use the stencil with watercolors and a paintbrush to put the design on place cards or other decorations for your Thanksgiving table. Let dry.

Mable

Nelia

5. Make another turkey stencil just for food items. Set the clean stencil carefully on a cake, pumpkin pie, or brownies, and lightly sprinkle powdered sugar over the stencil. Carefully lift the stencil to show the powdered sugar design.

Indian Corn and Gourd Paper Chain

Corn was an important food crop for the Wampanoag. Indian corn did not look like the light yellow corn we now buy in grocery stores. Indian corn kernels came in different colors of yellow, red, brown, and even blue.

What you will need

- pencil
- tracing paper
- construction paper
- markers or crayons
- scissors

Gourds are related to squash and melons. They have a tough, woody rind, or skin. They were used by the Wampanoag to make cups, dishes, bowls, and other useful things.

WHAT TO DO

1. Use a pencil and tracing paper to transfer the patterns from page 38 to the construction paper.

2. Color the patterns as you wish.

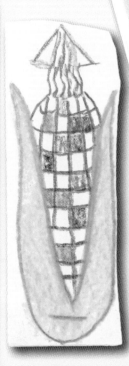

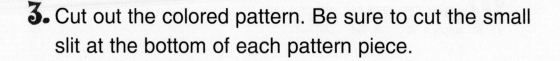

3. Cut out the colored pattern. Be sure to cut the small slit at the bottom of each pattern piece.

4. Fold in the sides of the arrow point of the pattern and slip the point through the slit of another pattern piece.

5. Open the folded points so that the arrow holds the pattern in place.

6. Make enough pieces to form a chain.

"I Am Thankful for My Family" Tree Sculpture

Families and friends like to get together on Thanksgiving Day. Statistics show that more people travel for the Thanksgiving holiday than any other time of the year. It is a great time to visit with family and friends.

What you will need

- pencil
- tracing paper
- light cardboard
- brown poster paint
- crayons or markers (optional)
- scissors
- green construction paper
- white glue
- photographs or drawings of family and friends (Ask permission first for photographs.)
- clear tape

WHAT TO DO

1. Use a pencil and tracing paper to transfer the tree trunk and base patterns to the light cardboard. See page 42 for the patterns.

2. Paint the trunk and base with brown poster paint or color it with crayons or markers. Let dry.

3. Cut out both the tree trunk and base. On the trunk, cut a slit from the bottom as shown by the green line in the pattern. Cut a slit on the base as shown by the brown line.

4. Use tracing paper and a pencil to transfer the leaf pattern to the green construction paper. See page 42 for the patterns.

5. Glue the leaves to the branches of the tree. Let dry.

6. Glue photos or drawings of family and friends on the trunk and leaves. Let dry. If you do not have photos or drawings, write a name on each leaf.

7. Put the trunk and base together by slipping the slit on the bottom of the trunk into the slit on the top of the base.

8. Put clear tape along the line where the trunk and base meet.

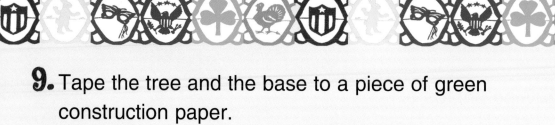

9. Tape the tree and the base to a piece of green construction paper.

"What I Am Thankful For" Mobile

Have you ever thought about those things that you are most thankful for? What are they? Some things might be family, parents, grandparents, brothers, sisters, home, health, friends, food, freedom, school, church, and many more. This mobile is a nice way to share with your family the things you are thankful for.

What You Will Need

- construction paper— 12 x 18 inches
- scissors
- tracing paper
- markers or crayons
- clear tape
- string
- wooden dowel

WHAT TO DO

1. Cut the 12 x 18-inch construction paper into two pieces that are 3 x 18 inches.

2. Fold each 3 x 18-inch piece of paper in half so that the short sides meet. Fold it in half again.

34

3. Cut a rectangular window that is 2 x 3½ inches into the folded construction paper. Be sure to cut through all the layers of paper.

4. Cut the tracing paper into eight rectangles that are 2½ x 4 inches. Use a marker or crayon to write a word or draw a picture of something you are thankful for on the tracing paper.

5. Tape the tracing paper rectangles on the inside of the construction paper over the openings. Be sure the words are facing the right way for the finished project.

6. Tape the ends of the construction paper together. Gently pinch each fold of the construction paper so that it forms a box with four even corners.

7. Cut two pieces of string 14 inches long. Tape the ends of the strings to opposite sides inside each box. Tie the strings to a 12-inch long dowel.

8. Tie a 12-inch string to the middle of the 12-inch dowel. Have an adult help you hang the mobile.

PATTERNS

The percentages included on the patterns tell you how much to enlarge or shrink the image using a copier. Most copiers and printers have an adjustable size/percentage feature to change the size of an image when you print it. After you print the patterns to their true sizes, cut them out or use tracing paper to copy them. Ask an adult to help you trace and cut the shapes.

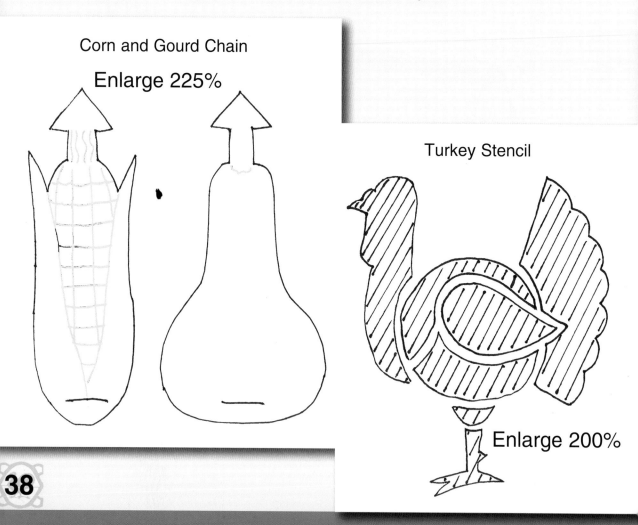

Corn and Gourd Chain

Enlarge 225%

Turkey Stencil

Enlarge 200%

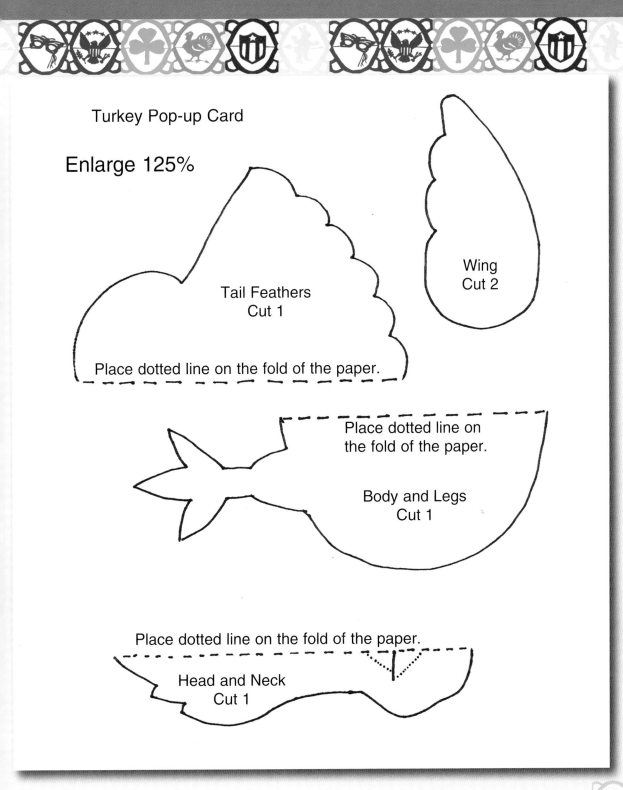

Turkey Pop-up Card

Enlarge 125%

Tail Feathers
Cut 1

Wing
Cut 2

Place dotted line on the fold of the paper.

Place dotted line on
the fold of the paper.

Body and Legs
Cut 1

Place dotted line on the fold of the paper.

Head and Neck
Cut 1

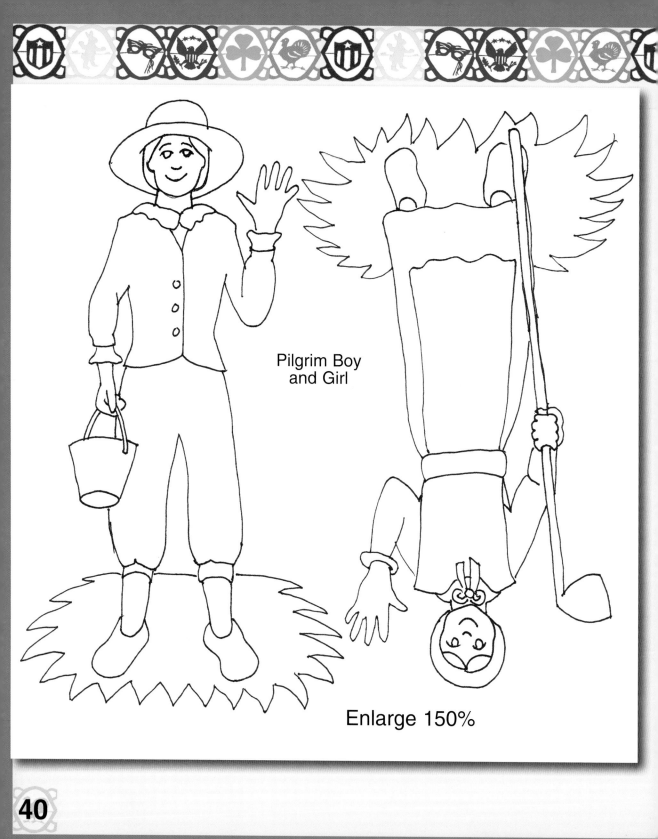

Pilgrim Boy
and Girl

Enlarge 150%

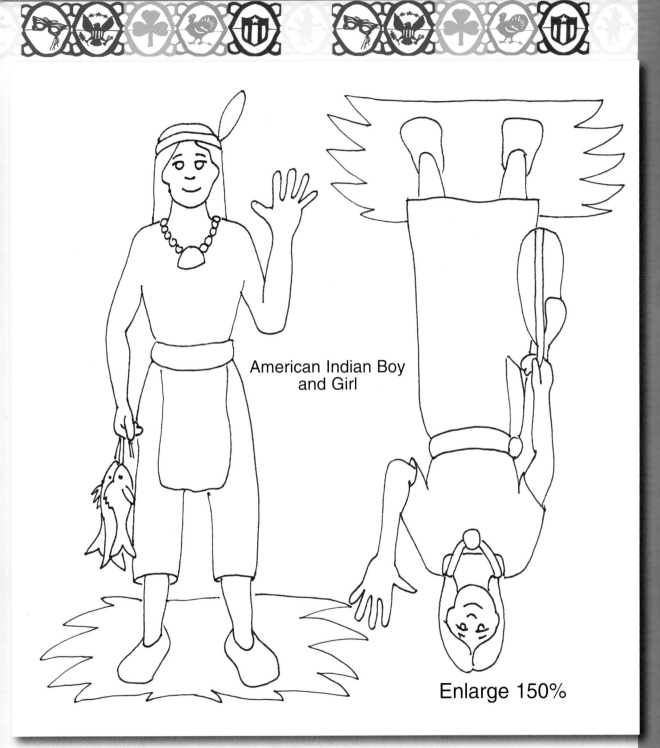

American Indian Boy
and Girl

Enlarge 150%

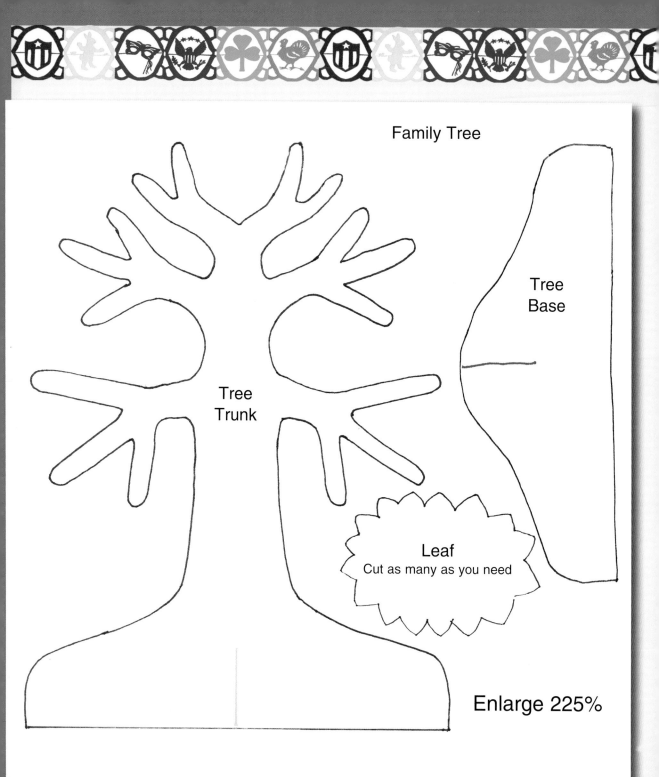

Family Tree

Tree
Base

Tree
Trunk

Leaf
Cut as many as you need

Enlarge 225%

HAPPY THANKSGIVING

READ ABOUT

Books

Englar, Mary. *The Pilgrims and the First Thanksgiving.* Mankato, Minn.: Capstone Press, 2007.

Heinrichs, Ann. *Thanksgiving.* Chanhassen, Minn.: Child's World, 2006.

Peppas, Lynn. *Thanksgiving.* New York: Crabtree Pub. Company, 2009.

Prelutsky, Jack. *It's Thanksgiving!* New York: HarperCollins, 2007.

Internet Addresses

Kaboose: Thanksgiving 2010

<http://holidays.kaboose.com/thanksgiving/>

National Geographic Kids:
First Thanksgiving

<http://kids.nationalgeographic.com/
    kids/stories/history/first-thanksgiving/>

DLTK's: Thanksgiving Crafts

<http://www.dltk-holidays.com/
    thanksgiving/crafts.html>

Visit Randel McGee's Web site at
<http://www.mcgeeproductions.com>

45

INDEX

ABOUT THE AUTHOR

Randel McGee has been playing with paper and scissors for as long as he can remember. As soon as he was able to get a library card, he would go to the library and find the books that showed paper crafts, check them out, take them home, and try almost every craft in the book. He still checks out books on paper crafts at the library, but he also buys books to add to his own library and researches paper-craft sites on the Internet.

McGee says, "I begin by making copies of simple crafts or designs I see in books. Once I get the idea of how something is made, I begin to make changes to make the designs more personal. After a lot of trial and error, I find ways to do something new and different that is all my own. That's when the fun begins!"

McGee has also liked singing and acting from a young age. He graduated from college with a degree in children's theater and specialized in puppetry. After college, he taught himself ventriloquism and started performing at libraries and schools with a friendly dragon puppet named Groark. "Randel McGee and Groark" have toured throughout the

United States and Asia, sharing their fun shows with young and old alike. Groark is the star of two award-winning video series for elementary school students on character education: *Getting Along With Groark* and *The Six Pillars of Character.*

In the 1990s, McGee combined his love of making things with paper with  his love of telling stories. He tells stories while making pictures cut from paper to illustrate the tales he tells. The famous author Hans Christian Andersen also made cut-paper pictures when he told stories. McGee portrays Andersen in storytelling performances around the world.

Besides performing and making things, McGee, with the help of his wife, Marsha, likes showing librarians, teachers, fellow artists, and children the fun and educational experiences they can have with paper crafts, storytelling, drama, and puppetry. Randel McGee has belonged to the Guild of American Papercutters, the National Storytelling Network, and the International Ventriloquists' Association. He has been a regional director for the Puppeteers of America, Inc., and past president of UNIMA-USA, an international puppetry organization. He has been active in working with children and scouts in his community and church for many years. He and his wife live in California. They are the parents of five grown children who are all talented artists and performers.